Ava & Carol Detective Agency
Rainforest Animal Guide

Thomas Lockhaven

Twisted Key publishing

2020

Copyright © 2020 by Twisted Key Publishing, LLC

All rights reserved. No portion of this book may be reproduced, stored in a retrieval system, or transmitted in any form or by any means - electronic, mechanical, photo copy, recording, scanning, digitally, or other - except for brief quotations and critical reviews or articles, without the prior written permission of the publisher.

First Printing: 2020

ISBN 978-1-947744-54-7

Twisted Key Publishing, LLC

www.twistedkeypublishing.com

Ordering Information: Special discounts are available on quantity purchases by corporations, associations, educators, and others. For details, contact the publisher at the above listed address.

U.S. trade bookstores and wholesalers: Please contact Twisted Key Publishing, LLC by email twistedkeypublishing@gmail.com.

CONTENTS

Amazon whipsnake......... 3

Assassin Bug................. 5

Bullet Ant..................... 7

Caiman......................... 9

Eyelash Viper............... 11

Golden Poison Frog...... 13

Goliath birdeater.......... 15

Howler monkey............. 19

Jaguar.......................... 21

Leafcutter ant............... 25

Leech........................... 29

Macaw.......................... 33

Piranha......................... 37

Scolopendra.................. 41

Spider monkeys............. 45

Tanagers....................... 49

Unicorn Mantis.............. 51

Wandering Spider.......... 55

Whiteknee tarantula..... 59

Zombie ants.................. 61

In Ava and Carol's new adventure, *The Curse of the Red Devil*, they travel to the Amazon Rainforest to attend Camp Adventura in Brazil. This book looks at some of the exciting wildlife they discover in the jungle.

Ava and Carol's adventure takes place in the Amazon Rainforest in South America.

The Amazon is a wet lush environment filled with thousands of amazing creatures. The rainforest is made up of four different layers. Many animals spend their entire lives in one layer, while others move from layer to layer.

If we work our way from the top of the rainforest to the bottom, it would look like this:

The top layer is called the **Emergent Layer**. This layer is made up of the tallest trees, like the Brazil nut tree and is home to animals like the Scarlet Macaw and the Harpy Eagle.

The second layer is the **Canopy Layer**; it is made up of the lush leaves and branches of the trees and is home to howler monkeys, spider monkeys, bats and insects, flying frogs and many types of birds.

The third layer is the **Understory Layer**; it's filled with smaller trees, such as the banana trees and coffee trees. The understory is also filled with lush vegetation, spiraling vines and orchids and poinsettias. You'll find the eyelash viper, butterflies and the Honduran white bat here.

The fourth layer is the **Forest Floor**, which is made up of roots, leaves, ferns, fungi and leafy vegetation. You'll also find many predatory and dangerous animals here such as the jaguar, poison dart frog, Goliath bird-eating tarantula, wandering spider, bullet ants, lizards and rodents.

Let's take a look at some of the amazing creatures from Ava and Carol's adventure!

Amazon Whipsnake

The Amazon Whipsnake is also known as the Machete Savane. They are large, slender, non-venomous snakes that are known for their passive (non-aggressive) behavior. They're considered intelligent hunters that search for their prey in shrubs and trees.

They are beautiful snakes. Their belly is often a bright shade of yellow or orange, their body can be from dark brown to yellow or gold. The tail is usually darker than the body. Many have a light-colored stripe that runs down the length of their body.

Lifespan
10-12 years

What do they eat?
They feed mostly on frogs, but they'll also dine on lizards and birds.

How long are they when fully grown?
About 10 feet. The height of a basketball rim.

Assassin Bug

The Assassin bug is the vampire of the rainforest. If you thought mosquitoes were bad, this charming insect uses its hollow proboscis (a fancy name for nose) to pierce and inject toxins into its prey, and then slurp up their liquefied insides like a protein shake. Needless to say, assassin bugs have a difficult time making friends.

Size
0.16in - 1.57in

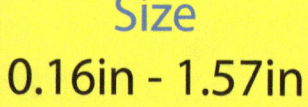

Diet
Insects, insects and more insects. There are few types of assassin bugs that are parasitic and feed on mammalian blood. Ticks are another example of a parasitic insect.

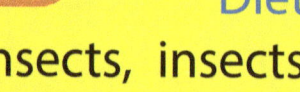

Life Expectancy
In captivity, they have been known to live as long as 2 years—but it's not known how long they live in the wild.

Natural Enemies
Birds, rodents, praying mantis, spiders, other assassin bugs and bowling balls.

Do they have a painful bite?
Yes, their bite is painful, however, it's usually not harmful to humans, unless they are carrying Changas disease. Changas disease can cause heart failure and cause organ damage. It's bad news however if you are an insect. Once bitten, a cockroach will live about 2 seconds, a caterpillar up to 10 seconds.

Weird Fact
The ant snatching assassin bug hides itself under a pile of its dead prey and then ambushes insects when they come near to investigate.

Bullet Ant

Bullet ants are synonymous with the word ouch. Well actually ouch's bigger brother, Yee Ouch! People that are bitten by this large ant describe the bite as feeling like they've been shot. According to the Schmidt pain scale for stinging and biting insects, the bullet ant gets a 4+. The plus isn't because he's an overachiever, it's because the bite hurts so badly.

Wait a minute, just a four? Yes, I had the same reaction. The Schmidt scale is a four-point system, developed by Dr. Schmidt who has been bitten and stung over a thousand times in the name of science. To put things in perspective, a honey bee sting receives a two.

Size
0.7in - 1.2in
They are big ants!

What do they eat?
Bullet Ants are omnivores, they eat termites, crickets, katydids, worms, spiders, flies, centipedes, small insects, nectar and tree sap.

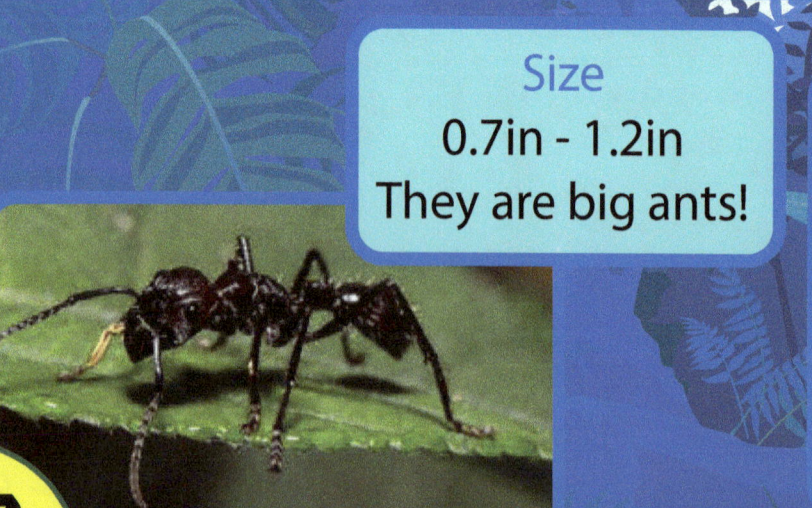

Bonus: What was the most painful sting?
The Tarantula Hawk Wasp

The pain from a bullet ant bite can last up to 24 hours and include fun things like waves of excruciating pain, temporary paralysis and uncontrollable shaking where the bite occurred. You mean if I got bit in the kitchen, my kitchen would shake? No, I'm talking about on your body. If the ant bit your hand, then your hand would shake, says the author shaking his head. No, I did not get bitten on my head.

Weirdness Factor

The indigenous Satere Mawe tribe in Brazil uses bullet ants in their coming of age ceremony. Young boys cannot become men, until they go through a ritual where their hands are placed in gloves filled with hundreds of bullet ants. They must keep their hands in the gloves for at least five minutes. To complete their initiation, they must do this twenty times.

Where do they live?

They live in colonies like most ants. Their favorite place in the rainforest is at the base of trees.

Caiman

Caiman are members of the Alligatoridae family. They're not nearly as well-known as the common crocodile or alligator. They may need a new publicist. Unlike their relatives, the alligator and crocodile, they don't pose a threat to humans. Most are too small, except for the Black Caiman which can reach up to nearly twenty feet and weigh up to nine hundred pounds.

Caiman live in rivers, marshes, swamps and lakes. Most Caiman like freshwater. If it's a long, hot, dry summer, they will go into a summer hibernation called an aestivation.

Aestivation

Prolonged dormancy of an animal during a hot or dry period.

Weird but cool

Caiman's eyes reflect a brilliant ruby red at night if you shine a flashlight at them.

Lifespan

30-40 years

What's on the menu

Fish, small mammals, birds, dinosaurs (aha, seeing if you were paying attention)

Communication

Caiman communicate through bellows, growls. Some Caiman if threatened will inflate their bodies and hiss like a leaky tire to frighten away predators.

Eyelash Viper

DANGER METER

First, I'll address the elephant in the room. How did they get this unique name?

Eyelash vipers get their names from enlarged scales over their eyes that resemble…you guessed it, eyelashes.

Just because they have a cute name, doesn't mean they're not dangerous. They're not aggressive, but the eyelash viper is considered one of the most dangerous of venomous snakes. The viper's fangs release a hemotoxic venom to kill their prey. Hemotoxic venom destroys red blood cells, disrupts blood clotting and can cause organ failure. The eyelash viper's bite can be fatal to humans.

The eyelash viper lives in trees and is a relatively small snake, only about twenty inches when fully grown. They have heat pits below their eyes that help them with hunting.

Speaking of hunting, what do they like to eat?
An eyelash viper's diet consists of lizards, small birds, reptiles and mice. Like many snakes, it swallows its prey whole.

Who is this guy afraid of?
Other snakes, birds of prey, humans

Lifespan in the Wild
Up to 10 years

Lifespan in Captivity
Up to 20 years

Golden Poison Frog

The Golden Poison Frog's bright yellow skin is a warning to predators. Don't eat me, I'm poisonous. This is a reoccurring theme in nature. Many times, brightly-colored animals are nature's way of informing other creatures that what they are about to eat is poisonous.

Lifespan
10 years

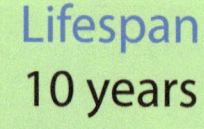

How big are they?
They're tiny but potent. Golden Poison Frogs can be anywhere from an inch to two inches.

Poison tree frogs belong in the "admire, don't touch" category. A single tree frog has enough venom in its skin to kill 10 people. Indigenous tribes use the Golden Poison Frog's poison to hunt. You're probably wondering how they could do that safely. The natives hold the tree frog with a waxy leaf, that protects them from the frog's toxin, and they rub the tip of their blowgun dart on the frog's skin. They shoot the dart from their blowguns to shoot small prey like rabbits.

Weirdness Factor

Did you know that poison frogs bred in captivity are not poisonous? Scientists believe that the frogs get their venom by eating poisonous insects and plants.

Goliath Birdeater

The Goliath Bird-Eating Spider or GBES, is the world's largest spider, and he has the biceps to prove it. Actually, I don't think spiders have biceps, but if he did, they would be huge. I'm sure. Goliath Spiders can weigh up to a half a pound. If you were to take their legs and spread them out, it would equal the size of a dinner plate, about 11 inches.

These spiders are a type of tarantula, and when they are confronted by a predator, they rub and release fine hairs from their abdomen. These hairs irritate the eyes, nose and mouths of would-be attackers.

Female Lifespan
15-25 years

Males aren't so lucky
Lifespan: 3-6 years
Sorry guys.

Massive Ouch Factor
Goliath Spiders have massive fangs, up to 1.5 inches long. That's two gummy bears stacked on top of each other. Their bite however is worse than their venom, which is considered mild and not harmful to humans.

Weirdness

Contrary to their name, they rarely ever feast on birds, they rely on much easier prey, like elephants. I'm just kidding of course. So, what do they eat? These guys love to eat worms, insects, amphibians and if they happen to come across a very slow-moving bird, then yes, this majestic spider will live up to its name.

For such a large spider, their natural camouflage is amazing. Can you find the spider in this picture?

Attack!

Goliath Spiders are ambush spiders. They love to hide out in marshes, swamps and wet grounds. They burrow into the soft soil, and wait. Since their eyesight isn't very good, they rely on the sensitive hairs on its legs to pick up the vibrations of approaching prey. Once it draws near, the spider will explode from its burrow and attack.

Bon Appetite

In South America, the local tribes roast Goliath Spiders in banana leaves and eat them. Yum!

Howler Monkey

Want to take a guess why they're called Howler Monkeys? Take your time, I'll wait. If you said they're called Howler Monkeys because of their incredibly loud vocalizations, you would be correct. Their calls are so loud that they can be heard up to three miles away. Who needs a cell phone when you've got a voice like that!

Howler monkeys howl from the time they wake up until they go to sleep. They use their loud voice to communicate with their troop or to warn other animals to stay away. Their howl is sometimes compared to a lion's roar.

Howler monkeys are covered in dense fur all over their bodies except for their face, and have a long powerful tail. They make their homes in the canopy level of the Rainforest.

What do they like to eat?
Howler Monkeys are herbivores, meaning they don't eat meat. They eat leaves, fruit, berries, flowers and nuts. Occasionally, they have been known to eat bird eggs.

How big are they?
Howler monkeys, when fully grown, weigh about 20lbs, and can be anywhere from 1½ - 3 feet.

Lifespan
15-20 years

Weird Fact
They use their tail as a fifth hand. They have what is called a prehensile tail, which is a special tail that has adapted to grasp, hold and manipulate objects.

Jaguar

Although they may look cuddly with their tan fur and black markings, these apex hunters are all business, and lack a sense of humor. During the day, jaguars enjoy sprawling on tree limbs in the shade, but at night, they become stealthy hunters. The word Jaguar comes from the Native American word Yaguar, which means, he who kills with one leap.

Jaguars are the third largest cat in the world and are powerful swimmers. So, if you think you're going to jump in the Amazon River and swim away, think again. Jaguars have been known to dive into the water attacking caimans and turtles.

Jaguars usually have one to four cubs. The babies are able to start tromping through the rainforest with their mom when they are about eight weeks old. During this time, she will teach them the skills they need to survive on their own. Jaguar cubs usually leave to go on their own when there are two years of age.

Lifespan
12-15 years

How big are they?

Jaguars are usually around 6½ feet from nose to tail and can weigh anywhere from 123 to 212 pounds.

What do they eat?

Jaguars are carnivores, so they'll eat just about anything they can catch. Deer, sloths, monkeys, birds, tapirs, caiman, dinosaurs. There you go with the dinosaurs again….

Biteforce
200 pounds per square inch

Leafcutter Ant

If you're ever looking for a pair of scissors and can't find a pair, try a leafcutter ant instead. Though small, they are mighty. A colony of leafcutter ants can defoliate (remove all the leaves) from a eucalyptus tree in one night.

Now you are probably asking yourself, what could these ants possible do with these leaves? If you're not, I'll wait while you do so.

Leafcutter ants are herbivores and eat a special kind of fungus. This fungus just happens to need decaying leaves to grow.

Size
1/8inch - 5/8inch

Leafcutting is not a one person—scratch that—ant job, it takes an entire colony. There are three sizes of leafcutter ants. The maxima, is the largest. Its job is to explore and find suitable vegetation to defoliate. The media, is medium-sized, it cuts the leaves into pieces with its powerful mandibles and drops them to the ground. Minima, the smallest, take them underground to a special location.

The media, also helps to carry the leaves to their colony, where they chew the leaves until they are soft and gooey. The fungus feeds on the decaying leaf goo. The minima are like farmers, they tend to the fungus and keep it healthy.

Media ants have a groove on top of their head to help hold the leaves they cut down. Carrying the leaves on their backs also protects them from predators.

What do they eat?
Lepiotaceae fungus

Cool fact
Leafcutter ants have mandibles that look like a saw blade. Their jaws can vibrate 1000 times a second, enabling their serrated mandibles to easily cut through the stem of a leaf.

Strong little insects

They can carry twenty times their bodyweight. To put this into perspective, the average human can carry about ½ to full bodyweight for short distances. The strongest human in the world Hafthor Bjornsson, currently weighs 395 pounds and just broke the deadlift record by lifting 1104 pounds, a little over 3 times his bodyweight.

Lifespan
3-5 weeks

Leech

Leeches are adorable. Just look at that face. Okay, I tried, but I think most people have the idea that all leeches are blood-sucking creatures that attack anything or anyone that happens to enter their territory isn't true. In North America, there are quite a few freshwater leeches that don't feed on blood, they feed on decaying vegetation, worms and insects.

So, which leeches do we see in movies or on animals? Hematophagous are blood-feeding leeches. These leeches will attach their suckers to mammals, reptiles, fish, even birds. Thankfully, their bites are not dangerous, or painful.

How can you say they aren't painful?

When a leech attaches itself, it releases an anesthetic which numbs or desensitizes the area. They also release an anticoagulant called hirudin, that stops the blood from clotting. Once they are full, leeches detach themselves, without so much as a goodbye or a thank you.

Leeches can be an expensive date, they can eat up to five times their own weight. However, the good news is, many leeches can go up to a year without food.

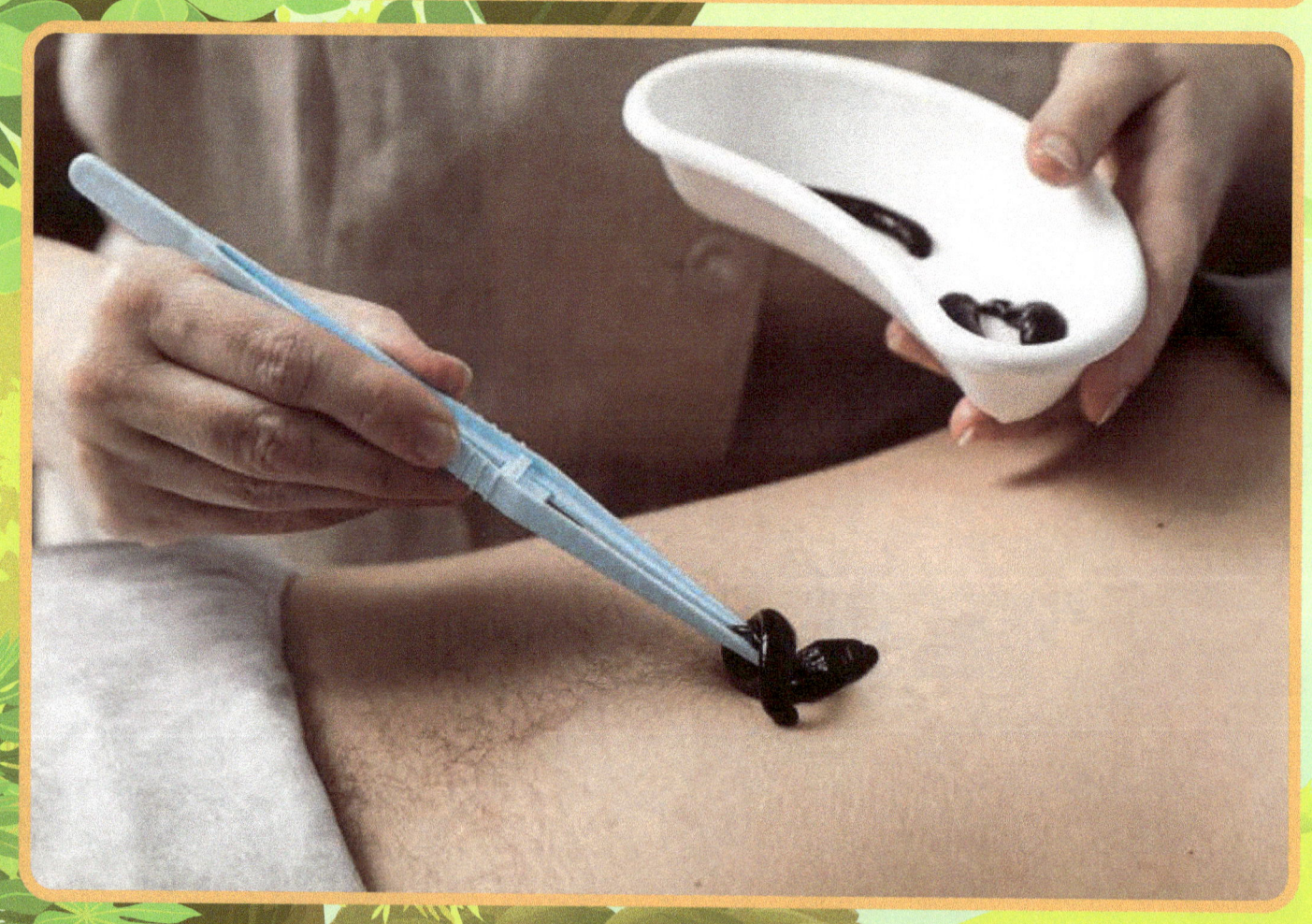

Leeches have been used in medicine for centuries, but don't expect to see one in a lab coat and stethoscope any time soon. Leeches are applied to surgical sites to make use of their blood-vessel cleaning abilities.

The giant Amazon Leech can grow up to 18 inches and live ten years. It's proboscis (nose) can be up to six inches long.

Weird Fact 1
Some people keep leeches as pets, and they allow the leeches to feed on them.

Lifespan
Up to 10 years

Weird Fact 2
Leeches have 32 brains. Their internal structure is divided into 32 segments, and each segment has its own brain and can work independently.

Macaw

There are several macaws living in the rainforest like the Hyacinth (Blue) Macaw and the Scarlet Macaw.
If you saw the Disney movie Rio, then you've been introduced to the extraordinary Blue Macaw. There are very few Blue Macaws left in the wild. Sadly, they are on the verge of extinction due to poachers and animal smugglers. A Hyacinth Macaw can be sold from ten thousand to forty thousand dollars to wealthy collectors.

Blue Macaws can be mostly found in the Emergent and Canopy layers, flying above the trees chatting nosily with one another. These beautiful birds can grow up to three feet and are the largest bird in the macaw family.

Macaws are extremely smart and have the ability to problem solve. Their intelligence level is said to be equivalent to a human toddler. Macaws in captivity have been known to unlock their cages with ease. They use their extremely powerful beaks to climb—maneuvering upward branch by branch, and to crack open hard-shelled nuts. Their beaks are so powerful they can crack open a coconut. Their biteforce is 200 pounds per square inch. For a comparison, humans have a bite force of 162 pounds per square inch.

Yep, she's a keeper!

Macaws are one of the few animals that have the same mate for life. Unlike my family, these romantic birds share their food with each other.

What do they eat?

Macaws eat seeds, nuts, fruits, flowers, leaves, snails and stems

Masters of Mimicry
Macaws can mimic the human voice and other noises in their surroundings.

Lifespan in the Wild
50-60 years

Lifespan in Captivity
60+ years

Weirdness Factor
The blue macaw has a very interesting tongue. It's black with bright yellow stripes. It also has a bone in it that helps them extract the nuts out of shells.

Piranha

The word piranha literally means "tooth fish," in local dialect. President Teddy Roosevelt vilified piranhas in his book "Through the Brazilian Wilderness" when he described them as merciless killing machines. If piranhas could read, I am sure they would have been quite offended. Piranhas usually don't attack humans, and some are even vegetarians, like the red-bellied piranhas.

What do they eat?

Piranhas are omnivores. They eat insects, fish, crustaceans, worms, carrion (dead animal), seeds and fruit. Piranhas are also cannibals. They eat their own species and will eat other piranhas if no other meat sources are available.

So, when do piranhas attack?

Piranhas are attracted to loud noises, splashing and blood. Speaking of blood, like sharks, they have special sensory organs that enable them to sniff out a single drop of blood in fifty gallons of water. Piranhas usually attack in groups, not for strength, but for safety. When they attack, they go for the prey's eyes or tail, to immobilize them.

Lifespan in the Wild
10 years

Lifespan in Captivity
Up to 20 years

Piranhas have an extremely powerful bite, seventy-two pounds per square inch, that's 3 times their bodyweight. According to National Geographic, relative to its body size, this is the strongest bite ever recorded by a fish. The shape of their teeth is like a sawblade. Local tribes use the teeth to make weapons and tools.

How big are they?

There are so many different types that there is a huge range in size. They can range from five to twenty inches in length.

Weird Fact

If another fish is eyeballing them, they will make a noise that sounds like a dog barking. It's their way of telling the other fish to buzz off!

Scolopendra

If you're a fan of extremely large centipedes, then you're going to love the Scolopendra Gigantea. It's the largest species of centipede on the planet. They are carnivores with voracious appetites and are prey to very few predators, or archnemesis.

Lifespan
10 years

Who would dare challenge this miniature tank on wheels? A tiny, but extremely venomous Arachnida, the Brazilian Yellow Scorpion. They usually attack while the mother Scolopendra is busy guarding her eggs.

Scolopendra have a pair of modified front legs (forcipules) that serve as fangs, which connect to venom glands located beneath their head, and mandibles that are used for seizing and killing prey. They will hunt and eat virtually anything that they are able to overpower, that includes other arthropods (invertebrate animal such as insects and spiders), amphibians, mammals, reptiles, frogs, snakes and mice. Scolopendra have been known to scale cave walls and attack and kill bats.

Scolopendra Gigantea bites are painful and their venom is a mix of histamine, serotonin, cardiotoxin, and a quinoline alkaloid. This venomous cocktail can cause severe pain, fever, chills, convulsions and anaphylaxis (a life threatening, severe, allergic reaction—similar to people with peanut or bee allergies).

Scolopendra Fangs / Forcipules

The Scolopendra sheds its skin like a snake so it can grow larger. Most grow up to 9 – 10 inches. There have been a few found that have been over a foot long. They breathe through spiracles (holes in its outer shell).

Spider monkeys

What kind of key opens a banana?
A monkey.

Why did the monkey like the banana?
Because it had appeal!

Who doesn't love a good monkey joke? Alright, onward!

On average, they reach up to 22 pounds

Lifespan in the Wild
24-27 years

Lifespan in Captivity
Up to 40 years

Spider monkeys are members of the genus Ateles, which means, incomplete. Fortunately, they don't know how to read, or I'm sure they would be upset. They are considered incomplete because they don't have a thumb. However, in its place, they do have a very long and very talented prehensile tail which helps them balance and move through trees with ease.

Author Note

Never send the thumbs-up emoji to a Spider Monkey, they find it offensive.

How did they get the name Spider Monkey?

When they hang between branches with their arms and legs extended, and their tail wrapped around another branch, they look like giant spiders dangling in the trees.

What do they eat?
Nuts, fruits, seeds and berries

Spider Monkeys live in the high canopy level of the rainforest and rarely ever come down to the jungle floor. Spider monkeys are very social animals. They typically live in mixed groups of females, babies, juvenile and adult monkeys—with about 15 to 25 individuals in each group.

Endangered

The black-headed and brown spider monkey are critically endangered. This is a result of locals hunting them for food and deforestation.

Tanagers

Just like in the movie Karate Kid Part II, where Mr. Miyagi catches a fly with his chopsticks, Tanagers pluck insects out of the sky as they fly by. Talk about fast food!

Tanagers come in many colors: yellow, red, green, blue, black—most are a mix of these colors. Males are more vibrant than females and juveniles.

While snapping your lunch out of thin air is exciting, tanagers also snatch insects off branches, leaves and from holes in trees.

Flocks of tanagers can be extremely diverse. At any given time you mays see up to 20 different tanager species flying or feeding together.

Diet

They have quite a diverse diet, not only do they feed on insects, but they also feast on a wide variety of fruits, berries, leaves, flower and nectar. Because of the wide spectrum of seeds they consume, tanagers play an important role dispersing seeds—through their poop—for trees and shrubs throughout the rainforest.

Lifespan
12-17 years

Size

There is a vast variety of tanagers that live in the rainforest. They can range anywhere from 3½ in - 7 in and weigh from ½ ounce - 1½ ounces.

Unicorn Mantis

You can now say that unicorns exist! Yes! Pump your fist in the air. The Unicorn Praying Mantis is a new species found in the Brazilian Rainforest, named for its hornlike appendage on its head. Scientists aren't sure why the praying mantis has a horn, they speculate that it's for mimicry or camouflage.

Size
0.5in - 6in

Lifespan
6 months

Why are they called praying mantis?

They get that name from the way they hold their extremely powerful spikey arms against their bodies; it looks like they are praying. Those spikes by the way, are used to impale and hold their prey in place once they attack them.

Praying mantises are ambush hunters and can blend in with their environment by looking like a stem on a bush, or a leaf. They can swivel their heads 180 degrees and they have two large compound eyes and three smaller eyes located on the center of their head to help them hunt. Their powerful legs are so fast, that their attack is too fast to be seen by the human eye.

What do they like to eat?
Crickets, moths, caterpillars, flies and grasshoppers

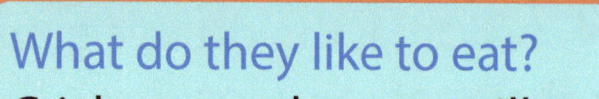

While researching for this book, numerous sources said that the praying mantis will only eat live insects. However, many people that own praying mantises have uploaded videos of them eating bananas and honey. Here's a YouTube video of a praying mantis chowing down on a banana: tinyurl.com/mantisbanana

Weird Fact

Run for your life! After mating, 15% of females consume the male. This is a time to strongly practice the saying, let's just be friends.

Wandering Spider

The Wandering Spider—not to be confused with the Wondering Spider, who's extremely inquisitive and is often found in quiet areas reading—has the honor of being the world's most venomous spider. I'll wait a moment while you applaud. Wandering Spiders belong to the genus Phoneutria which means murderess in Greek.

The wandering spider is also called the banana spider, because it is commonly found in clusters of bananas and hiding in banana trees. According to my extensive sources, the Wandering Spider does not like the moniker banana spider as it's not menacing enough.

Wandering spiders do not build webs, they roam the jungle floor at night in search of prey. During the day, they hide under rocks, logs or banana plants. When they attack, they bite down releasing a powerful neurotoxin that kills their prey within seconds. People that have been bitten by this spider suffer intense pain, problems breathing and loss of muscle control, which if not treated can lead to death.

When threatened, the wandering wpider will stand up on its hind legs, thrust its front legs into the air and rock back and forth from side to side—displaying their red fangs. Their fangs aren't really red, they are covered in a reddish-colored hair that makes them appear red.

Lifespan
1-2 years

How big are they?
Their body is about two inches, with a leg span of six inches

Whiteknee tarantula

The Brazilian whiteknee tarantula is an extremely fast grower. Within two to three years, it will triple in size, when fully grown, it can have up to a 9-inch leg span. It gets its name from the white bands on its legs.

What do they like to eat?
Lizards, crickets and small rodents like mice

The whiteknee tarantula is skittish; however, when it attacks, it attacks with unbridled ferocity. When their prey comes near, they will literally jump on it, wrapping their legs around it, until it succumbs to its attack.

Female Lifespan
Up to 20 years

Male Lifespan
Up to 4 years
Sorry guys.

When threatened, the whiteknee tarantula doesn't hesitate to use a subtle weapon, urticating hairs. Urticating hairs have miniscule barbs on them that work their way into the eyes, nose, mouth of the predator. These hairs are extremely irritating and painful.

Zombie Ants

What exactly is a zombie?

According to the dictionary, a zombie is a will-less and speechless human held to have died and been supernaturally reanimated (restored to life). While some aspects are true, others are not. First, zombie ants were not dead, and then brought to life. Normal, living ants succumb to a fungus called Cordyceps. This parasitic fungus grows through the ant's body creating a network of filaments that take over the insect's muscles and brain.

Once infected, the doomed ant is compelled to climb upward, until it reaches the perfect spot for the fungus to grow and flourish. Once it has reached its optimum destination, the ant will clamp down onto the leaf or branch with its mandibles and die. Eventually, the fungus sends a long stalk through the ant's body and grows into a bulbous capsule full of spores, which are then released into the jungle, starting the process all over again.

What are spores?

Spores are microscopic biological particles that allow fungus to reproduce. Think of them as tiny little seeds that you can't see without a microscope.

Run for your lives! The fungus is so powerful, so virulent (infectious, severely harmful) that it can wipe out an entire colony of ants. If an ant is found to have been infected, worker ants will take that ant far away from the colony.

Does the cordyceps fungus attack other creatures?

Yes, there are literally thousands of cordyceps that attack different creatures like spiders, moths, grasshoppers, scorpions and praying mantises.

Why do they attack these insects?

First, they need the insect's body to grow, and to place the fungus in an optimal location to best spread its spores. Second, scientists believe that the cordyceps fungus keeps the insect world in check by making sure a specific group doesn't grow too big.

New Book Releases

Thank you for reading *Ava & Carol Detective Agency: Rainforest Animal Guide*! This book is the companion guide of *The Curse of the Red Devil*.

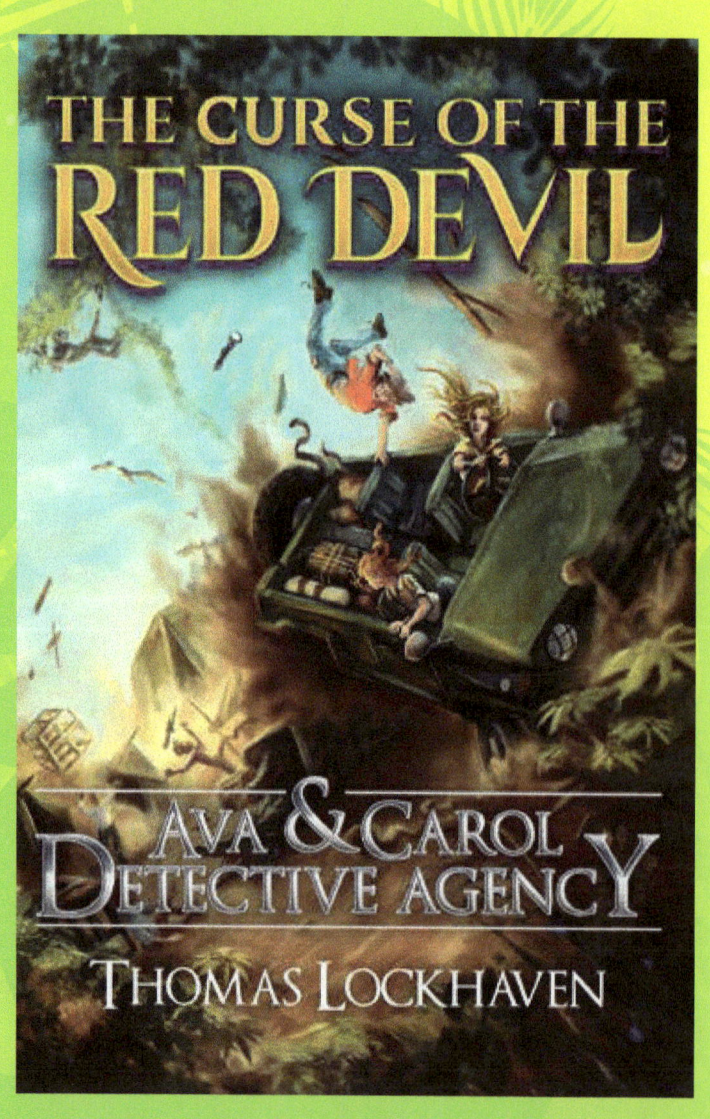

Sign up for our newsletter to learn of new book releases at avaandcarol.com

You may also follow Thomas Lockhaven's author page on Amazon or Bookbub.

Be sure to check out our exciting books in the action-packed series.

Book 1: The Mystery of the Pharaoh's Diamonds
Book 2: The Mystery of Solomon's Ring
Book 3: The Haunted Mansion
Book 4: Dognapped
Book 5: The Eye of God
Book 6: The Crown Jewels Mystery
Book 7: The Curse of the Red Devil